UNBECOMING

by laura muensterer

unbecoming
by Laura Muensterer

ISBNs: 978-1-953625-26-7 Trade Paperback
        978-1-953625-27-4 Hardcover
        978-1-953625-28-1 Ebook

kelley *creative*
SPOKANE · WA · USA

unbecoming is a story about healing. Forgiveness. And ultimately, salvation.

Salvation from oneself and self-limiting beliefs.

Detachment from societal expectations while creating new standards to live by.

In time, the mask falls off and you see who you are for the first time.

You become the highest version of yourself and reconnect with the divine.

With these lessons, you realize that you have always been free.

There is no greater journey than unbecoming everything you have been taught to be.

maybe this is what life is about
finding a way to be your own partner
your own best friend

she is starting to feel like home again
she is starting to feel like the person
i've been waiting for all along

Introduction

*In Buddhism, there are four stages of enlightenment —
Sotāpanna, Sakadāgāmī, Anāgāmī, and Arahant.*

*During each stage, universal themes of selflessness,
impermanence, and dissatisfaction underline changes
in one's behavior and overall outlook on life.*

This is my story of enlightenment.

I. Sotāpanna

When you embark on your journey to enlightenment, you discover there is no separation between what's in your head and what you see through your eyes.

You look within and search for a separate being, but you do not find a "self."

You realize it is all an illusion.

who am i?
a damaged soul

struggling to make sense
of things
beyond her control

i'm a house with four walls
but no stable foundation

the floor creaks
the faucets run
the pipes leak

and yet i find comfort
in knowing i built it
all on my own

i keep searching
searching
searching for answers
a reason
a cause

but there's nothing to grab
or hold on to

so i continue on this journey
looking for something tangible
physical
real

that i can point to
and say
"that's why i am the way i am"

i wish i could know
all the answers

and discover
all the truths

but instead
i wander this world

looking for love
in unforgiving places

the whispers of sadness
are knocking again

the problem is
i am too eager
to let them in

every day
i wonder

am i helping myself
or simply preventing love
from flowing to me?

the sky sighs
i can feel its sorrow

hoping for happiness
to awaken it tomorrow

i am a wave
of endless concern

reaching the shore
only to find

no destination
to rest my mind
in sight

find me in empty hallways
where the light peeks in
and the sun welcomes a new day

the wind blows outside
but indoors
i am all alone

here i patiently wait
for peace of mind
to reach me

like a seam coming undone
my emotions burst
through my skin

exploding into a dialogue
of despair
that prevents me

from ever coming
up for air

the taste of regret
leaves my lips

i wipe it off
with the little bit of life
i have left

i am the ghosts in the graveyard
the shadows in the hallway

haunting time with every breath
stirring in endless thoughts

and hiding from reality
with every step

i keep trying to run away
from the world that shaped me

the world that turned me
into the person i am

maybe it's because
that version of me
no longer exists

yet she continues to persist
in the reality she tried so hard
to escape from

i keep finding myself back
in the same place i started

revisiting these wounds and scars
with fresh eyes
and a more open heart

so i close my eyes
and imagine a world
in which i start all over

no pain
no sadness
no marks on my name

my body is stained
with memories

i hold on to them tightly
as if i don't carry them

with every fiber of my being
one day they will

no longer be
a part of me

i fell hard
not for love

but for the possibility
that someone

could quiet my mind
better than i could
on my own

when you're all mental
getting outside your head
is like a vacation

for just a few minutes
you're in the present moment

it is incredibly fleeting
but so unbelievably freeing

i have an obsession with patterns
if i can notice them
from the very beginning

maybe i can put an end
to this unforgiving cycle
i continue to find myself in

words beg to
escape my mouth

i stuff them back
down my throat

and consume them
like they are my last meal

tomorrow there will be
nothing left to feel

because i have felt my feelings
and they no longer feel real

why is it
that when love

finds me
comforts me
warms me

the urge to retreat
overpowers me?

i am merely a shell
of a person
a holograph of a girl

maybe one day
i will be real
in this world

where to find me?
in a black hole perhaps
disappearing into an abyss maybe

wherever i am
the destination is always

far from the security
of a tangible reality

between seconds
i rest in intervals

moments in time
barely recognizable
to the naked eye

there are not good days
nor bad

there are simply days
blending into one another

oh how i wish
i could feel a break
between these subtle lines

despite my sorrows
regrets
and betrayals

the love in me
persists

like a light
that cannot be
turned off

i patiently wait
for my problems
to destroy me

because in my heart
i know

destruction will lead
to resurrection

II. Sakadāgāmī

As your journey continues, you stop attaching yourself to what is outside of you.

You accept negative emotion and do not let it hold you back anymore.

You start to stand in your power.

you look at me
and i flinch

how am i supposed
to open up

when i can barely make sense
of this disorganized mind?

i am a tidal wave reaching shore
slowly but surely
i make my way to the edge

the edge of insanity?
potentially peace?
the water can only know

so i tread lightly
on my toes
where the water goes
i go

there is no end in sight
i am simply floating
as time passes me by

a fire inside me burns
as people use it
to warm their own bodies

leaving me nothing
but dying flames

i have learned
to protect this fire
from those who see it

as a place to receive
and never reciprocate

i wipe the dust
off distant memories

and embrace lessons
i learned

before releasing them
back into the unknown

i constantly stare
at the woman
in front of me

and wonder
can she see

she is the love
she ultimately seeks?

before
i was drowning

now i am simply
a fish in an endless ocean

searching for the next destination
to call home

i wander aimlessly
into the cosmos

hoping to find solace
in the lack of truth

found in this
limitless reality

what happens when
the things you have
not said or healed

have no body
to claim as their own?

what happens when
your endless cycle
of thoughts

has no mind
to call home?

maybe they simply float
into the air

as if they were never
even there

i am simply a cloud
floating into mindless oblivion

madness is what i'm drawn to
chaos is what i crave

intimacy
comforting one day
poisonous the next

it either fills you up
or prevents you
from feeling whole

this is why
i must now let go

so i pull away
like i've done countless times

pretending there are no emotions to feel
no future to be built
no conversations to be had

maybe in our next life together
i'll have the courage to

speak up about
what i think is real

this body of mine
is not what it seems

it is a hollow place
filled with
forgotten memories

words fall flat
they no longer carry
any meaning

maybe tomorrow
i will feel more
than a connotation

so i will tend
to my wounds
on my own

without expecting anything
in return

from the people
who caused them

with every goodbye
i feel the ache of endings

until a new beginning
pulls me out of my sorrow

and reminds me
there is always tomorrow

what do i crave?
a warm body next to me at night

the freedom to do
whatever my heart desires

but most importantly i yearn for
the ability to calm my restless mind

there is a fine line
between love and lust

i have walked this line
many times

searching for a resolution
a message in the stars

there is never any answer
beyond my intuition telling me
to keep moving on

it's a tragedy
we hold so much space
for people

yet they leave us begging
for simply a seat
at their table

i have died
so many times
i don't even know
if i'm truly alive

tell me
how can i
be surrounded by

so many people
yet feel
no souls?

there is ice in my veins
snow on my soul

waiting for someone
to bring me in
from the cold

i wander through each year
holding onto questions and fear

hoping to one day
put my stresses to rest

gently lay them
down on the bed

tuck them in tightly
and say goodbye

as I walk away
from the pain
they have caused me

i am trying so hard to be good
good to what?

myself, maybe
the world in its entirety

the words i say
the actions i take

reflect the sacrifices
i'm willing to make

the world will dump
its problems onto you

if you're not careful
you may find yourself

drowning in issues
that were never yours
to solve

it's okay to be soft
as long as you
do not let your softness

let people treat you
like you're less than them

your ability to be kind and nurture
does not give others permission
to take advantage of your empathy

as i've gotten older
life has become
a balancing act

choosing to flow
instead of force

deciding to plan
instead of react

and saying "no"
while learning
how to let things go

III. Anāgāmī

Negative emotions and habits fall away. You find peace within yourself and no longer fear the unknown.

You accept your circumstances and begin to enjoy life.

You no longer feel a void inside of you.

i want so badly
for someone to tell me
i am doing everything right

now that i realize
there is no voice
to be heard

i have learned to become
my own source
of reassurance

i'm soaring through the cosmos
wandering through the world
traveling in peace

knowing the universe
is always protecting me

from anyone and anything
that does not serve me

i no longer let the wind take me
to vast forests
of the unknown

i am my own compass with
intention behind every action
strategy behind every step

by living this way
i know i will reach my goals
and always put myself first

i am skilled at enduring
persisting
moving without expectation

i am not holding my breath wondering
what comes next

i am simply letting the universe guide me
to wherever i am supposed to land

i have learned
self-doubt is nothing but fear
disguised as a helping hand

i will no longer take this hand
and let it lead me astray

the growth i have been cultivating
is only a few steps away

wandering around the world
has become routine for me

instead of fighting the inevitable
i have learned to shake its hand
and become its friend

i am learning to appreciate
the journey

and look forward
to the destination

every step i take
brings me closer
to becoming myself again

a girl who had
no worries on her shoulders

and who only held
love and forgiveness
in her unbroken heart

the older i get
the more i enjoy
my own company

how beautiful is it
that i can sit calmly

and appreciate the kindness
that was born
out of inner violence

solitude is the greatest gift
you can give yourself

in moments of stillness
you discover parts of yourself

that when uncovered
unlock a world of possibilities

what do i want?
a soft place to land

when i fall back
into bad habits

a place to rest my head
when the world gets heavy

but overall
all i really want

is to leave this world
better than i found it

i ached for stability
trying to find peace
around every corner

over the years
i've learned
there is no masterpiece to create

the beauty of life
is found in the imperfections
of our routine lives

behind closed doors
the truth set me free

like a bird
escaping a cage
that bound her to unhappiness

i have escaped many times
each time finding my wings freer
than before

i am learning to
welcome the darkness

invite it into my softness
and transform it into a portal of light

that reveals where i need healing
so i can live without fear

and foster happiness
within myself

so i continue to travel
with my heart
in my hand

and my head
in the clouds

as the candle
stops burning

the wax dries
the smoke subsides

i see clearly
for the very first time

while i learn from these lessons
i get closer to understanding
the value of love and logic

for they always lead me
to uncharted territories
of self-discovery

whenever i judge others
i realize
i am only judging myself

they are showing me
what i have refused to accept
so i can confront discomfort

and learn to appreciate
the darkness and light

that live in harmony
within my body

the best thing i ever did
was choose to befriend my mind
instead fighting it all the time

the conversations i had
became a lot lighter
breathing became a bit easier

and i no longer allow
fears and insecurities
be more than moments in time

love can be unforgiving
leaving you feeling alone

despite this possibility
i do not let it stop me
from uncovering someone's soul

for each person i meet
teaches me about the value
of being on my own

the only way to stop a repeating cycle
is to reach deep inside yourself
and realize your self-worth

once you find it
you can never unsee it

this self-discovery
provides everything you need
to set yourself free

IV. Arahant

Wholeness reaches you and inner bliss fills each day.

You experience a sense of completeness and enjoy a new perspective on life.

You are now enlightened.

i waited so long
for someone to save me

searching far and wide
to one day realize

she was following
right behind me
the whole time

i am no longer
a victim of my thoughts
a servant of my mind

the thoughts i think
the actions i take

are a representation
of my ability
to remain awake

the emotions i crave
can be created at any time

there is no limit
to my connection
with the divine

my true power
lies in my ability

to trust my decisions
follow my instincts

and let my intuition
lead me to gardens
filled with beautiful possibilities

my heart has been stepped on
my love has been thrown away

but somehow
i am still able to say

it was worth it
in every possible way

i will never underestimate
the power of my mind

everything i desire
is already mine

a light follows me
tracing my every step

i look behind me and see
a whole sun
rooting for me

soon
i will fly so high

i will no longer
be able to see the sky

everything that has happened
has either been a lesson
or a blessing

i do not live with any regrets
because i know that everything is happening
for my highest good

and the universe never gives me challenges
that i cannot overcome

as the smoke rises
uncertainty disappears

and i discover
who i have been
all these years

i forgive myself
for not honoring the credit I deserved

i forgive myself
for forgetting my peace is the priority

now that I know my worth
no one can ever take it away from me

you cannot water
dead flowers
and expect them
to grow

he didn't give me
what i wanted
which set me free

it taught me
the only person
i can truly depend on
is me

to help yourself
feel whole

you must let go
of the misperception

that you were never
complete on your own

when asked
what i've learned
through the years

it's hard to say
with just words

yet easier to show you
through the forgiveness
i now eagerly give away

if you were
to hold my heart

you would feel
the weight of the world

yet I continue to walk
this unforgiving path

like a bird traveling
through endless clouds

carrying nothing but hope
on her shoulders

i have reached rock bottom many times
each time discovering
a deeper well of sadness
waiting for me

whenever i climb out of this well
i have found even greater reasons
to keep going

even more inspiration
around each corner
and more motivation
than i have ever seen before

my soul no longer cries
my mind no longer fights
my body no longer aches

i have become one with the universe
and no longer wait for others
to help me feel whole

slowly but surely
i reconstruct my life

like flowers in a garden
i lay down new soil

from which i harvest
my infinite potential

every day i am learning
smarter ways
to take care of myself

so that no matter what happens
i can always find a safe place to retreat
inside of me

a secure place to heal the trauma
that has held me back
from tapping into the potential
the universe has provided me

i worry less
and trust more

i forgive
and later forget

my stresses subtly
start to fall away

as i enjoy new blessings
each day

i will no longer apologize
for who i am

i will no longer abstain
from speaking my mind

i will no longer nibble
at what sets my soul on fire

i will devour it like it is
the only way to stay alive

my cup is brimming
with beautiful potential
seeds ready to soar

and blossoms filled
with everything i want
and more

and so i cry
not because i am sad

but because
i am so overjoyed

with the blessings
that are coming toward me

nothing is sweeter
than the revenge of

being who you are
with no apology
or shame

this is
who i am

curious
confident
chaos

and i love myself more
every day

my eyes are filled
with possibilities

when i look in the mirror
all i can see

is infinite opportunities
waiting for me

the chaos has subsided
the fears have disappeared

for the first time in years
love for myself
has finally appeared

About the Author

Laura Muensterer is an avid writer who uses creative storytelling to express her innermost thoughts, emotions, and fears about the world.

Through deep introspection and therapeutic intervention, Laura explores various aspects of the human experience while shedding light on the many ways our past shapes our present and future self.

www.lauramuensterer.com
@lnmpoems on Instagram